92
BAN   212502

AUTHOR
Allison, Amy, 1956
TITLE
Antonio Banderas $17.95

DATE DUE	BORROWER'S NAME	ROOM NUMBER

92
BAN   212502
   Allison, Amy, 1956-
      Antonio Banderas

                                 $17.95

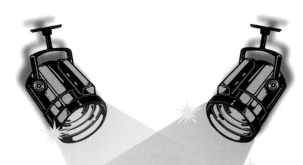

LATINOS IN THE LIMELIGHT

Christina Aguilera

Antonio Banderas

Jeff Bezos

Oscar De La Hoya

Cameron Díaz

Jennifer Lopez

Ricky Martin

Selena

CHELSEA HOUSE PUBLISHERS

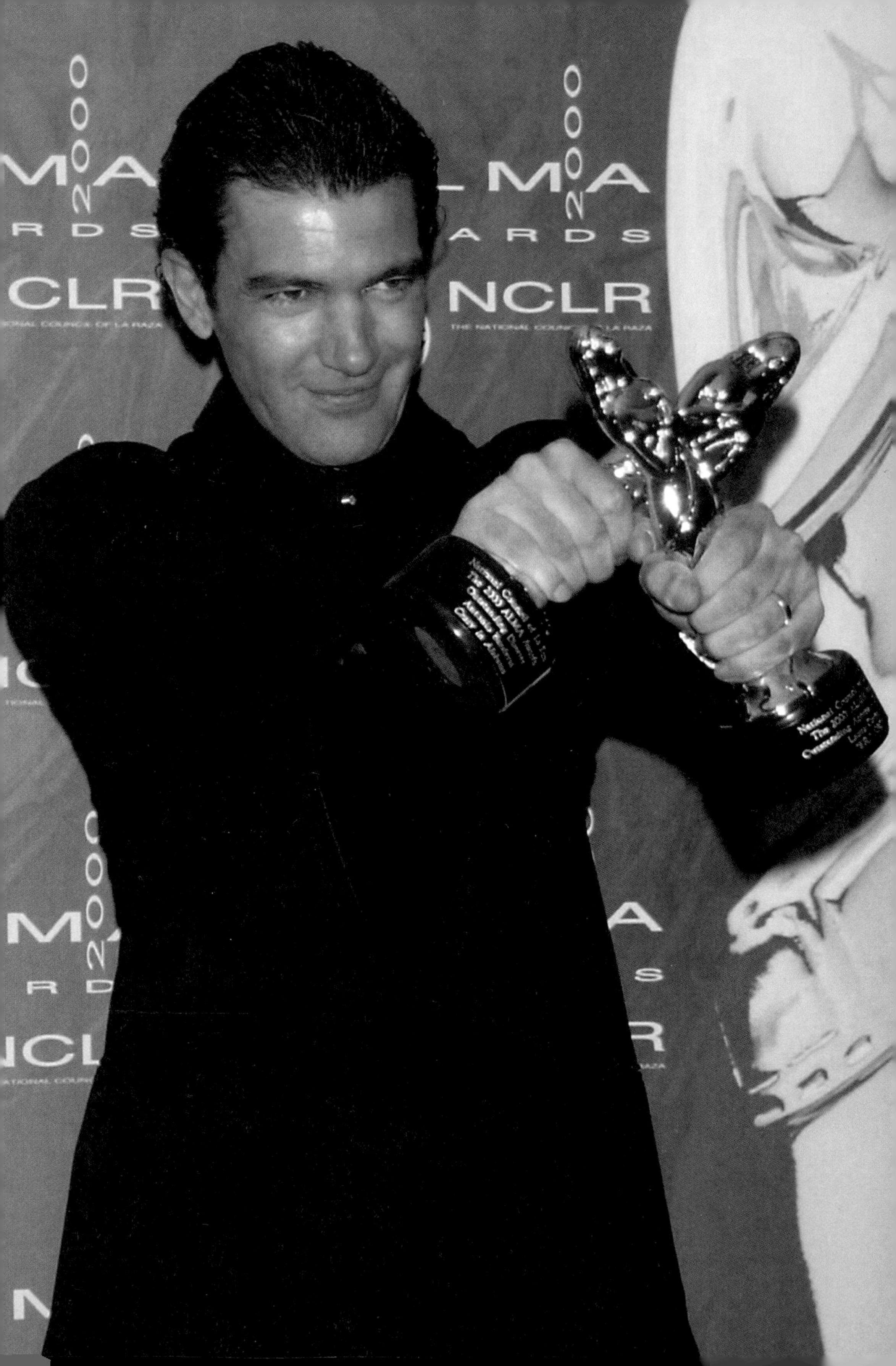
2000
NCLR

LATINOS
IN THE
LIMELIGHT

Antonio Banderas

Amy Allison

CHELSEA HOUSE PUBLISHERS
Philadelphia

Frontis: *Posing with two of his ALMA awards for acting and directing in April 2000, star of stage and screen Antonio Banderas has proved that a Latino actor can make it to the top in the film world.*

Produced by
21st Century Publishing and Communications, Inc.
New York, New York
http://www.21cpc.com

CHELSEA HOUSE PUBLISHERS

Editor in Chief: Sally Cheney
Production Manager: Pamela Loos
Art Director: Sara Davis
Director of Photography: Judy L. Hasday
Managing Editor: James D. Gallagher
Senior Production Editor: J. Christopher Higgins
Publishing Coordinator: James McAvoy
Project Editor: Anne Hill

The Chelsea House World Wide Web address is
http://www.chelseahouse.com

First Printing

1 3 5 7 9 8 6 4 2

Library of Congress Cataloging-in-Publication Data

Allison, Amy, 1956–
    Antonio Banderas / Amy Allison.
        p. cm. – (Latinos in the limelight)
    Includes filmography, bibliographical references, and index.
    ISBN 0-7910-6102-7 (hardcover) — ISBN 0-7910-6103-5 (pbk.)
        1. Banderas, Antonio—Juvenile literature 2. Motion picture actors and actresses—Spain—Biography—Juvenile literature. [1. Banderas, Antonio. 2. Actors and actresses.] I. Title. II. Series.

PN2788.B36 A44 2000
791.43'028'092—dc21
[B]   00—059631
                                                                 CIP
                                                                 AC

CONTENTS

CHAPTER 1
SWASHBUCKLING
TO STARDOM   7

CHAPTER 2
STAGESTRUCK   15

CHAPTER 3
THE BIG SCREEN   23

CHAPTER 4
SOULFUL SEX SYMBOL   31

CHAPTER 5
GOING HOLLYWOOD   39

CHAPTER 6
BEHIND THE CAMERA
AND BEYOND   49

CHRONOLOGY   59
FILMOGRAPHY   60
AWARDS   61
FURTHER READING   62
INDEX   63

SWASHBUCKLING
TO STARDOM

"My little sword won over all those fancy guns!" Antonio Banderas exclaimed. It was the summer of 1998, and *The Mask of Zorro*, an old-fashioned swashbuckler starring Antonio, had seized the number-one spot at the box office over special-effects spectaculars *Lethal Weapon IV* and *Armageddon*. What was even more surprising, however, was that when Antonio was tapped for the lead role in Hollywood's latest film featuring the action hero Zorro, the Spanish-born actor had not yet proved himself a box office attraction. Thanks to his leading-man status in a summer hit, Antonio now had star power.

The manner in which Antonio was selected for the lead in *The Mask of Zorro* was itself pure Hollywood. The hugely successful director Steven Spielberg approached Antonio at a party following the 1994 Academy Awards ceremony. Back in 1991, while watching the flashing swords in *Hook*, Spielberg remembered being spellbound as a kid by old movies, particularly the Zorro films. He was determined to produce a Zorro for the 1990s.

The first Zorro movie, the silent 1920 *The Mark of Zorro*,

Sword in hand, Antonio swashbuckled his way to stardom in The Mask of Zorro. *In the lead role of the dashing, romantic crusader for justice, Antonio fulfilled his dream of being the first Latino actor to play the well-known Hispanic hero, Zorro.*

catapulted Douglas Fairbanks into Hollywood superstardom. A 1940 remake made its lead, Tyrone Power, an idol in South America. Then in 1957, Walt Disney produced a Zorro TV series that won the character a new generation of fans. Kids scribbled Zs on their homework assignments, carried Zorro lunch boxes to school, and dressed up in Zorro's familiar black outfit, cape, and mask for Halloween. In the 1960s, the show was released in countries around the world, including Antonio's native Spain.

"I remember watching the TV series when I was a kid," Antonio says. "Sometimes I'd pick up a sword with my brother and we'd fight any terrorists we had in the South of Spain."

From early on, Antonio thought of Zorro as a hero. "[H]e's very alive and has strong principles and is very representative of the Spanish culture," Antonio comments about the character. "He has a very intense sense of loyalty." The actor, who's made no secret of his support for Spain's left-wing Socialist Workers' Party, adds: "Zorro in some ways has a very strong component of being a revolutionary. He's a man working for the people."

The heroic character of Zorro in fact inspired cartoonist Bob Kane to create Batman. Batman, like Zorro, has a dual identity as well as a passion for righting wrongs. Just as Batman is the alter ego of upscale businessman Bruce Wayne, Zorro is the wealthy aristocrat Don Diego de la Vega in disguise. And just as Wayne suits up as Batman to fight crime, de la Vega transforms himself into "The Fox" (the meaning of the Spanish word *zorro*) to defend the oppressed.

The Zorro character first appeared in 1919 as a five-part series in a pulp fiction magazine, *All Story Weekly*. The masked crusader for justice was the brainchild of a reporter from Illinois named Johnston McCulley, who saw his hero as a cross between Robin Hood and legendary Hispanic outlaws of the American West. These colorful figures resisted California's takeover by Anglo-Americans in the mid-1800s. Their heroic company included Salomon Maria Simeon Pico, who, like Zorro, rode at night and left a mark on his victims, and the charming, aristocratic Joaquin Murieta. According to legend, Murieta turned to banditry after Anglo-Americans stole his claim to a gold mine and attacked his family. He became a hero to his people after the U.S. government passed a tax discouraging those who were not natural-born citizens from pillaging California's gold fields.

The Mask of Zorro pays homage to the Murieta legend by naming one of its characters after the dashing outlaw. This character, Joaquin, and his younger brother, Alejandro—played by Antonio, are wily bandits in partnership with an Anglo. Legend links this Anglo's name, "Three-Fingered Jack," to Murieta's celebrated band.

The movie's action begins when the two orphaned Murieta brothers watch the heroic Zorro, played by Sir Anthony Hopkins, in an act of defiance. The year is 1821, and Spain's 300-year-old rule over Mexico is about to come to a crashing end. Peasants are in the streets protesting Spanish governor Don Rafael Montero's refusal to give up power before one last show of tyranny: the execution of a group of freedom fighters. Zorro, in reality Don Diego, rescues the prisoners and, with the help of the Murieta brothers, rides off unharmed. First, however, he rewards the older brother with a medallion from around his own neck.

When Don Diego next sees the medallion, a dirty and disheveled Alejandro is now grown and giving the medal, which he received from his dying brother, in payment for drinks. Alejandro is in despair after watching Captain Harrison Love and his band of California rangers shoot his older brother and Three-Fingered Jack. Don Diego convinces the hot-headed Alejandro that he can help the young man take his revenge.

Don Diego has revenge on his mind too—against Don Rafael, who is scheming to rule again in California. A family tragedy also impels Don Diego to seek vengeance. Many years before, Don Rafael was responsible for the death of Don Diego's wife before kidnapping Don Diego's baby daughter and sending Diego to prison. After 20 years, Don Diego has escaped his prison cell and wants revenge.

Don Diego's plan is to train Alejandro to replace him as Zorro, a hero the peasants still hope will fight for them against oppressors. "Zorro in our movie is much more a concept, really, than a personality. [It is] a concept that represents freedom, which represents responsibility," Antonio has explained, "So the man behind the mask, in this case me, is just a man learning."

One of the things Alejandro learns in the film is how to wield a sword. Antonio himself took lessons with the U.S. National Olympic Fencing Team to prepare for the role—and now has the scars to prove it. The film's fencing master, Bob Anderson, who dueled inside Darth Vader's suit in the *Star Wars* films and also trained such stars as Sean Connery, praised Antonio as "the best swordsman I have ever worked with."

Antonio is more modest about his ability. He explained that fighting for an hour with real swords kept him focused and feeling good, but added that after 14 hours of working he was a

lot less focused and ended up bloodied every day he had to fight with the sword. Following one scene during which Antonio crosses swords with 10 soldiers, director Martin Campbell says, blood was "running down his hands. I don't think he had a[n uncut] finger left."

As challenging as the dueling was in the film, it helped Antonio discover the key to Zorro as a hero. He felt that fighting with swords is not about strength but taking control of yourself. "[G]uns are cowardly," he told an interviewer. "With swords you need a confrontation, face to face. There is something about honor there." He added. "[I]t's not so aggressive for kids, in fact we took a lot of care about that."

Being slashed with a sword wasn't the only hardship Antonio endured during the making of *The Mask of Zorro*. In some locations in Mexico,

Antonio plays a scene with costars Anthony Hopkins (left) and Catherine Zeta-Jones, the woman he defends and romances in The Mask of Zorro. *Antonio had to learn swordfighting for the film, and he proved to be a talented pupil, drawing praise from his fencing master.*

Antonio appeared on the morning show Live with Regis and Kathie Lee *to promote the* The Mask of Zorro. *Antonio (left) and Regis Philbin (standing) enjoy a laugh over Kathie Lee Gifford, who took a tumble during a not-too-serious fencing match with Antonio while taping the show.*

where the film was shot, temperatures soared to 118 degrees. It was not just extreme heat that plagued the movie's cast and crew, however. The wind was incessantly blowing dirt, caking the cast members' nostrils and eyes with dust. In addition, some areas needed to be cleared of poisonous snakes each day before filming could begin. Still, in an interview included in the DVD release of *The Mask of Zorro*, Antonio pointed out the significance of shooting the movie in Mexico, where the culture supported his character's link to the Hispanic world.

The popular understanding of Zorro as a Hispanic superhero meant a lot to Antonio. In fact, he gave it as a main reason for signing on for the film because it gave the actor the opportunity to play one of the few Hispanic heroes Hollywood films have ever shown. The role also gave Antonio the chance to show his range as an actor. To prepare, he studied other actors' interpretations of the role and drew inspiration from each of them. Antonio played a scruffy outlaw, an aristocratic flirt, a gallant hero, and even a priest. "The devilish Banderas, the first Latin actor to play the role [on the big screen], blends all of the [styles of the actors who played Zorro before him] in his Zorro, rising to chandelier-swinging heights [Douglas] Fairbanks might envy," wrote an *Entertainment Weekly* reviewer.

Another *Entertainment Weekly* reporter, Lisa Schwartzbaum, commented, "Banderas keeps the romantic-hero stuff light, especially early in his apprenticeship when he flubs with a gangliness more usually seen among baby animals in Disney animation." Antonio enjoyed the lighthearted comedic side to his Zorro character who can laugh in the middle of a scary moment. The actor's ready humor clearly impressed journalist Garth Pearce, who noted that Antonio's eyes often projected a curious light that made it seem as if he were laughing while the rest of his face was serious.

Antonio even laughs off his sex-symbol image. His reply to host Billy Crystal calling him "The Sexiest Man Alive" on the 1993 Oscar broadcast was: "It's a joke, obviously." When he was listed as one of *People* magazine's 50 Most Beautiful People in the World for the first time in 1992 (he made the list again in 1994 and 1996), Antonio claimed he didn't always succeed with women. He recalled a time he dropped to one knee to announce his love for an approaching girl only to have her walk "right on by."

Of course he was just five years old at the time. He was already a kid with a very big imagination, however, and the world around him supplied plenty of fuel to fire his creativity.

2

STAGESTRUCK

Andalusia is Spain's most exotic region. This southern-most part of the country is known for some of the "hotter" elements of Spanish culture. It is famous for gazpacho, a spicy soup made from tomatoes and garlic. Andalusia boasts flamenco dancing, with its rhythmic hand clapping, foot stamping, and fiery musical accompaniment. The region is also the birthplace of one of the hottest actors of his time—José Antonio Dominguez—better known as Antonio Banderas.

At the time of Antonio's birth, his father, José Dominguez, worked as a customs officer. José's job was to inspect goods and passengers arriving and departing Spain through the Andalusian port town of Málaga. The famous artist Pablo Picasso was born just two blocks from the apartment building where José and his wife, Ana Bandera, made their home.

Ana, a schoolteacher, believes her family name "Bandera" goes back to the years between 711 and 1492. At that time, Andalusia was ruled by the Moors, a Muslim people from North Africa. Andalusia also included people of Spanish

---

Antonio's birthplace, Málaga, Spain, boasts a huge stadium, and the boy once dreamed of playing soccer there. After an accident kept him from the game, however, he discovered another passion—the theater—and began training for a future acting career that would make him an international performer.

15

descent and a large community of Jews. Given the mixing of races in the region, Antonio thinks it possible that Moorish or Jewish blood also runs in his veins.

When Antonio was born on August 10, 1960, Spain was controlled by the dictator Francisco Franco. At school Antonio and his classmates were forced to give the straight-armed salute associated with fascist governments. Even as a child, Antonio could not escape the oppressive feeling. He recalled that life under a dictatorship made him, and many other Spaniards, afraid to do or say anything controversial. Such fears made him shy. "I never called attention to myself. For example, at my Catholic school when we recited our prayers, I pitched my voice to sound exactly like the other students. I didn't want anyone to take special notice of me," he says.

Antonio first risked standing out from the crowd when he showed a talent for playing soccer. His skills earned him a place in the Guimbarda, a soccer team made up of boys from all walks of life and social classes in Spain. It was the first time that the middle-class Antonio had seen real poverty. One team member made a lasting impression on Antonio. The boy would hide away in a corner to change clothes after practice sessions. Antonio discovered that the boy's underpants, the only pair he owned, were full of holes. Later, when Antonio became an actor, he drew on the boy's silent pain to help interpret characters.

There were other poor kids on the team too. "I was told that their families had so little money that they had to go to work at 13 or 14. I then realized how hard my parents worked to provide for my younger brother, Francisco, and me," he says. The hardships of others also made

Antonio's parents, Ana and José Dominguez, were not so sure their starstruck son should pursue an acting career. But they finally relented and enrolled the teenager in drama school.

Antonio realize that the world out there was tough. Antonio experienced some tough luck himself when at 14 he broke his foot, ending his dreams of ever playing soccer professionally.

At about the same time, the boy discovered a new passion while watching a stage production of the musical *Hair*. "That night my mind exploded. It was like a religious thing to me," he later told a journalist. The energy and openness of the actors thrilled the teenager, and he realized that he wanted to express himself as the actors did. His announcement that he wanted to become an actor shocked his conservative parents. "I was like a weird animal in my family," Antonio says.

Antonio's soulful eyes and infectious smile belie the fact that he is dedicated to his chosen profession. As a young actor, he was totally serious about his career, working hard and learning all he could about the theater.

"I couldn't sleep at night, thinking I probably am crazy: What is this? To be an actor, this is not normal. This makes no sense."

Acting did make sense, however. Antonio had an active imagination that left the everyday world far behind. At eight years old, in an essay about a summer holiday spent with his aunt, he wrote about her house as if it were a haunted castle. He also liked to tell his boyhood friends horror stories, particularly at twilight. His mother also confirms that as a young teen, Antonio seemed distracted a lot of the time. He once slept with his boots on, and another time he showed up at school with the trash he was supposed to throw out. His mind was evidently elsewhere.

Finally recognizing Antonio's interests lay more outside the normal classroom than in it, his parents enrolled him in Málaga's School of Dramatic Art. Antonio's mother laid down one condition to his enrollment: He would study teaching as well as acting during his four years of drama school. However, the young teenager managed to get away with taking only one or two education classes a year. The rest of the time he spent learning the art of acting.

Antonio credits one of his acting teachers in particular with his ability to play a wide range of roles. Her name was Guillermina Solo. "She would tell us: 'It is like an opera: What is important is the music. It doesn't matter if I am a woman or a man—if I play the music [of the character], that's what people will see,'" he explains.

Antonio got plenty of chances to put Solo's acting advice into practice. Even before enrolling in the school, he was performing with Dintel, a local theater company that put on plays in a donated, broken-down old theater. The actors learned every part of theater craft—doing scenery, costumes, makeup, and lights. Often the players had to spend their own money to put on performances. Sometimes the troupe packed scenery in a truck and put on plays in little villages outside Málaga. They even performed in the streets, or wherever they could draw an audience.

Some members of the audience were not so welcome, however. The police kept a close watch on the group and stood ready to close down any play the Franco government found threatening. "We were doing theater against the regime, against Franco. It was part of a movement that

This is an undated photo of Spanish Dictator Francisco Franco. Under the Franco regime the police were directed to close down any plays that they found threatening to the government and to arrest the actors. On more than one occasion Antonio and his troupe were arrested and taken to the local police station for questioning.

was searching for democracy," Antonio recalls. "[T]he times were really an adventure. I remember doing a play and the cops would be waiting for us backstage with their helmets on, just shining. The curtain went down and you were taken to the police station."

Still, life with the theater company was not always so serious—not with Antonio around. The young actor was known for his practical jokes. Once he put a lot of vinegar and salt on a piece of bread a fellow actor had to eat onstage. In addition to being a comedian, Antonio was developing a reputation for living a charmed life. In fact, the other actors in Dintel nicknamed him "Breva," meaning "Lucky." He survived two motorcycle accidents during his years with the troupe. No sooner was his motorcycle repaired from the first accident than Antonio was eager to test its speed. He quickly revved it up to 75 miles per hour. Swerving to avoid a truck, he ended up flat on his face on the roadway, bruised and bleeding. It was days before he could move again.

Antonio seemed attracted to risk and was clearly out to prove himself. The big challenge came when Dintel's visiting director, Luis Belaguer, advised him to move to Madrid, Spain's capital, to pursue acting professionally. While it sounded like a great opportunity, Antonio hesitated. His mother was worried about him being on his own, and he became depressed and confused about what to do. Finally, he made up his mind, deciding that to pursue his dreams he had to leave home.

Just a week away from turning 20, Antonio left Málaga for Madrid. The $75 or so he had in his pockets when he left didn't last long. The only acting opportunities he could find were small roles in amateur productions. He held out for six months and then returned to Málaga.

"For three days I indulged my misery and self-doubts," Antonio later admitted. Fortunately for Antonio's future fans, that was not the end of the story. Remembering how he felt when he saw *Hair*, he emerged from that dark time and realized that acting was his passion and his vocation. He described his feelings: "It was that real calling that drove me forward. The intensity of my desire to act became the weapon that helped me conquer all the old fears."

Again, Antonio set out for Madrid. This time he was even more determined to make it.

3

THE BIG SCREEN

After the death of Spanish dictator Francisco Franco on November 20, 1975, the country's artistic community experienced a reawakening. Writers, directors, painters, and musicians made the most of their liberation from nearly 40 years of censorship and repression. They eagerly experimented with new subjects and styles. The center of this burst of artistic creativity, known as *La Movida* ("The Movement"), was Antonio's new home, Madrid.

"I was lucky that I got to Madrid just at that moment when everything was exploding," he says. "There were all these new designers, new directors, and young people working in music. Now that people were free to think out loud, the ideas wouldn't stop—it was a flood. The energy was incredible."

The buoyant energy of the time helped keep Antonio's hopes afloat as he went from audition to audition. To support himself between acting gigs—some of which did not even pay—he took a variety of jobs: waiting tables in a

Eager to enjoy Spain's new artistic creativity after the death of dictator Francisco Franco, Antonio entered the exciting theatrical world in Spain's capital city, Madrid. Proving his talent and versatility in a variety of theater roles, he drew the attention of Spain's leading filmmaker, Pedro Almodóvar, and soon the young actor was on his way to the silver screen.

pub, working as a salesperson in a department store, ushering at a theater, working the lights for a stage production. "The money I earned went to buy decent clothes for auditions and to pay for acting lessons," Antonio recalls. Often he could not even afford to ride a bus to auditions, and he walked, sometimes as far as six miles. While walking, he would look around on the street between parked cars, hoping someone had dropped some change he could pick up.

Finally, after about a year of scrounging for acting jobs, Antonio worked up the nerve to audition with Spain's National Theater. The director, Luis Pasqual, immediately sensed the young actor's promise. Still, Pasqual told Antonio that before he could offer the young hopeful a job, he would have to talk with the producers of the play he was casting. Antonio persisted, saying he needed an answer immediately—he had no other income at the time. Pasqual gave in, assuring Antonio he had passed the audition.

Acceptance into the National Theater meant that Antonio had succeeded as a professional actor in Spain. At the age of 21, he could count himself a member of the country's top acting troupe. In the wide variety of plays put on by the National Theater, Antonio developed his range as an actor, appearing in works from classical Greek tragedy to contemporary American drama.

One night in 1982 after a performance at the National, someone stopped by Antonio's dressing room. It was the filmmaker Pedro Almodóvar, who was then making a name for himself in Madrid. The city was swept up in *La Movida*, and Almodóvar's bold, original films fit right in with the movement's readiness to push the limits of what was acceptable in art. Antonio vividly remembers meeting Almodóvar for the first time: "He opened my dressing-room door and walked in, this wild, dirty underground director with a reputation for breaking all the rules. He asked if I wanted to make a movie. I said, 'Sure, what's it about?' He told me it was about a bunch of crazy people in Madrid.' I thought, *This guy is crazy or a genius*. Luckily for us, he was both."

Not only did Almodóvar offer Antonio a start in films, he also bestowed on Antonio his new professional name. Antonio had been considering the "stage" name Antonio Abascal, but Almodóvar convinced him to go with Banderas. The young actor liked the symbolism of modifying his mother's maiden name. For Antonio the name Banderas made a statement in support of Spain's move toward greater freedom and democracy. Antonio's enthusiasm for the "new" Spain connected him as a kindred spirit with Almodóvar.

Antonio showed a gift for expressing the right mix of seriousness and silliness for Almodóvar's films. The characters he played were generally sensitive young men driven by conflicting passions—making them tragic yet ridiculous at the same time. For example, in his film debut in Almodóvar's *Labyrinth of Passion*, Antonio was cast as an Iranian terrorist who falls for the son of the government leader he's sworn to overthrow. In the 1986 film *Matador*, feelings of guilt and shame brought on by his overly religious upbringing result in Anontio's character confessing to murders he did not commit.

The controversial subjects of these films —homosexuality, religious extremism, terrorism— were not lost on Antonio. "Almodóvar is a breaker," the actor says. "He arrived, giving the audience something new, something different, something very courageous. He's crying, yelling to the people, something very aggressive. Yet at the same time," Antonio adds, "he has a beautiful sense of humor too. He can tell you . . . the harshest story . . . and suddenly you are laughing and crying at the same time."

Starting out his movie career with a pioneering filmmaker was an exciting, although not always easy, time for Antonio. It was also not very lucrative. Antonio admitted that when he and Almodóvar began a film, they were never even sure they would finish it, let alone make any money. He also admitted that working with Almodóvar was no party. The director could be difficult, always demanding something new and fresh, and often even cruel, berating Antonio for his performance.

Nevertheless, working with such a demanding filmmaker had its rewards. Antonio called it something magical. Audiences seemed to agree. Acting in Almodóvar's films, Antonio became one of Spain's top performers. For his role in the 1990 Almodóvar release *Tie Me Up! Tie Me Down!* he received Spain's equivalent of an Academy Award nomination for best actor. The young performer's growing stardom made him a celebrity, not only in his native Spain but throughout Europe. Suddenly, all the major European magazines wanted him for their fashion pages.

Despite winning fame as a film star, Antonio had not given up on his stage career. He continued acting in plays at the National Theater. One day he walked into the café below the theater to grab a cup of coffee when he suddenly spotted a small, dark-haired woman. "There was something about her that I instantly understood,"

With actress Victoria Abril in Tie Me Up! Tie Me Down!, *Antonio displayed that magical quality that made him at the age of 30 one of Spain's top performers. As his stardom grew, so did his film offers and his celebrity throughout Europe.*

Antonio recalls. "I had to meet her." The woman, Ana Leza, was a fellow actor. She had seen the play Antonio was performing in at the time and was an admirer. They talked and began dating.

A smitten Antonio bought Ana flowers, wrote her poetry, and composed songs for her.

He has admitted that before meeting Ana, he only thought he was happy when he was being a bit crazy and having a good time with his friends. As he recalls after finding Ana, "Now I had someone I could share everything with, the good and the bad." In 1988, nine months after they first met, Antonio and Ana were married. Because of Antonio's busy acting schedule, he and Ana exchanged vows at a simple wedding ceremony in Madrid.

Nineteen eighty-eight was a significant year for Antonio professionally as well as personally. It marked the release of his most successful film to date, Almodóvar's *Women on the Verge of a Nervous Breakdown*. The plot of this zany film turns on a series of coincidences. For example, Antonio's character, Carlos, is considering moving into an apartment that belongs to a woman named Pepa, who his father has been seeing on the sly. Hidden behind glasses, Antonio plays the nerdy Carlos, who dutifully fixes Pepa's phone for her when he arrives to check out the apartment. Pepa has been using this same phone to try to contact Carlos's father, who has left a message on her answering machine breaking up with her.

The role of Carlos brought Antonio to the attention of audiences around the world. *Women on the Verge of a Nervous Breakdown*, which had the honor of being screened on opening night at the prestigious Cannes Film Festival, became an international hit. It even won an Academy Award nomination for Best Foreign Film of 1988.

The nomination brought Almodóvar and the film's cast to Los Angeles in March 1989. Almodóvar insisted they all attend the award ceremony together. Because the same group

of actors worked with Almodóvar on every film, they formed a kind of family. To the filmmaker, then, it seemed perfectly natural that his actors would go along with him to the Oscars.

Antonio recalls being excited to see all the Hollywood stars that night at the Oscar show. "It was a strange, strange experience," he says. "I remember looking out from the stage and seeing Liza Minelli, Jack Nicholson, and Kevin Costner, thinking, What am I doing here? This is not my place." Antonio would soon feel right at home with these legendary actors, however, for he was on his way to becoming just as successful.

With his role as the somewhat confused young Carlos in Women on the Verge of a Nervous Breakdown, *Antonio, here in a scene with actress Carmen Maura, starred in a film that became an international hit.*

4

SOULFUL SEX SYMBOL

In March 1992 *US* magazine dubbed Antonio "Spain's hottest export." That year the Spanish actor made his American film debut. Two years earlier he had received the call to meet with the film's director, Arne Glimcher, in London. Glimcher was planning to bring Oscar Hijuelos's prize-winning novel, *The Mambo Kings Play Songs of Love*, to the screen.

The novel tells the story of César and Nestor Castillo, two brothers who are also musicians. The brothers leave their native Cuba for New York City in the 1950s with dreams of making it big playing mambo, traditional Latin dance music. Antonio read the film's script on the plane to his meeting with Glimcher, and by the time the plane landed, he was definitely interested.

There was only one problem—Antonio did not speak English, and the director did not speak Spanish. "I kept making faces, going, 'Oh yeah . . . of course, right, right, right.' It was like a comedy," Antonio recalls. For his part, Glimcher says, "He was very good at grabbing my arm and laughing and smacking me on the back. This went on for about a half hour until I said, 'You don't understand a

Hollywood hailed Antonio as the new Latin sex symbol when he appeared as the trumpet-playing Nestor Castillo in his American film debut—The Mambo Kings.

word I'm saying, do you?' And he just smiled and laughed. Right then I knew I had my actor."

Before signing Antonio, Glimcher wanted him to take a screen test, which involved saying lines from the script in front of a camera. To prepare himself, Antonio hired a language coach to teach him the part he would be auditioning for—the role of the younger, trumpet-playing Castillo brother, Nestor. Antonio learned his lines phonetically (by sound), practicing them over and over. Still, the test was scary for Antonio because he did not really understand what he was saying.

Although Antonio passed the screen test, still another hurdle lay ahead for the Spanish-speaking actor. Because he had to learn English quickly, Glimcher immediately enrolled him in an English course. For eight hours a day, Antonio stammered through language training. Then, after studying English all day, he spent evenings learning how to finger the trumpet. He also had to learn to dance the mambo. That came easier. "Because I am Spanish," Antonio says, "I could sense something in the steps immediately."

In the six months Antonio worked on *The Mambo Kings* he found himself drawn to the United States. Like his character in the film who said so many times how much he loved America, Antonio too realized how much he cared about the country. At first, it was a bit frightening for the actor, and he felt as if he was beginning all over again. Still, he sensed that his future was in the United States.

His intuition proved true. "*The Mambo Kings* changed my life," Antonio said in 1994. "Since then, I've spent more time here in America than in my own country." He continued: "Never, ever am I going to have the words to thank Arne Glimcher, because of the way he trusted me and the way he took this risk. He was the key in the door of my career here in America."

And that career was taking off. Though *The Mambo Kings* fizzled at the box office, "it did introduce Banderas's brand of soulful masculinity to the American film industry," wrote journalist Margy Rochlin. Antonio's performance as the deeply emotional Nestor Castillo wowed a very important player in the movie business at the time. Director Jonathan Demme, hot off the Oscar-winning *Silence of the Lambs*, wanted Antonio for his next feature film.

The film, *Philadelphia*, starred Tom Hanks as Andrew Beckett, a homosexual lawyer intent on defending his professional reputation. Andrew sues his legal firm for firing him because he has AIDS. Antonio played Andrew's supportive life partner, Miguel, a role he was proud to take. He believed strongly in the film, which he felt talked openly about a tragedy in American society and that would help people understand the suffering of AIDS victims.

Philadelphia was a controversial film not only because it brought to life society's fears about AIDS, but because it also confronted people's unease with homosexuals. One way the film sought to overturn negative stereotypes was with the character of Miguel. "If we want people to accept Tom Hanks as gay and pull for him as a hero," director Demme explained, "then we better have a wonderful, wonderful boyfriend for him."

Demme believed Antonio was the perfect choice to play Miguel because the actor's "appeal cuts across all preferences." Demme echoed

Antonio in a scene with Tom Hanks (right) from the critically acclaimed film Philadelphia. *As Hanks's life partner, Antonio took on a controversial role, but one in which he strongly believed. Playing a homosexual also helped Antonio downplay his image as a sexy Latin lover.*

Antonio's previous director, Arne Glimcher, who characterized the actor as one with whom men, women, and even children could fall in love. *Philadelphia*'s casting director, Howard Feuer, described Antonio's appeal this way: "A lot of people look good, but Antonio has so much more—the intelligent twinkle in his eye and that incredible warmth. You look at him, and he gets you right in the heart."

Playing up the sex-symbol angle, newspapers and magazines from the *Los Angeles Times* to *Cosmopolitan* heralded the actor as a Valentino for the 1990s. Rudolph Valentino was a legendary Hollywood star who heated up the screen in the 1920s. The exotically handsome Valentino was the first of Hollywood's so-called

Latin lovers, who was followed by others, including Ramón Navarro, Ricardo Montalbán, and Fernando Lamas.

Labeling an actor a "Latin lover" is one way the film industry packages stars, and Antonio is well aware of this. He realizes that Hollywood is trying to stereotype him when he comments, "I'll probably be seen as that Latin Lover type forever. Even if I get greasy and fat and lose my hair, they'll cast me and say, 'Yes, but he was a Latin Lover!'" At the same time, he disagrees that the roles he has played fit the mold of the macho Latin male manufactured by Hollywood. Antonio has explained that his role in *The Mambo Kings* was not that of a Latin lover but of an insecure, sensitive, and introverted young man.

Antonio also broke the mold in his other U.S. film appearance in 1993, when he played a South American rebel in *The House of the Spirits*. One reviewer praised Antonio for making his role as a fiery Latin activist much more than just a stock character. Adapted from the widely praised novel by Chilean author Isabel Allende and starring Oscar winners Meryl Streep and Jeremy Irons, the film held high hopes for all involved. Those hopes were dashed when the $25-million production took a nosedive at the box office.

Still, Antonio was proud to be a part of the film because he was impressed by its subject matter. "It's a movie talking about freedom, talking about an era in South America where the people were very conscious of political events, the dictatorships," Antonio says. Recalling his experience growing up under Francisco Franco's iron rule, he says that the film reminded him of his native country's past.

The film industry, however, is only interested in history that pays off at the box office. Fortunately for Antonio's future in Hollywood, his next movie, *Interview with the Vampire*, was a commercial success. Antonio includes himself among the many fans of horror writer Anne Rice, on whose book the film was based. "I like the way she describes her characters, it's very deep and dark," he explains.

Critics agreed that even in his brief appearance on screen, Antonio powerfully expressed the torment of his character, Armand, the world's oldest vampire. He received glowing reviews for his characterization, which did not surprise the cast and the crew. In addition to his good looks, they cited his personality as a significant contribution to the film's success. According to the film's casting director, Juliet Taylor, "Some people get the English down, but they lose their heart. They are never able to convey their essential great quality in English. Antonio doesn't have that problem."

Indeed, Antonio seemed to be on the verge of joining the handful of non-native English-speaking actors to achieve Hollywood stardom —Ingrid Bergman, Sophia Loren, and Arnold Schwarzenegger among them. He has humbly acknowledged that he knew he would have to start from the beginning if he were to make his mark in Hollywood. Starting over meant accepting small, supporting roles for the first few years, and he claimed he would rather take his time to achieve stardom, keeping both feet on the ground.

Starting out also meant that Antonio would have to adjust to living in a new and different country. Despite his exceptional grasp of the English language, the young actor admitted

Despite his intelligent acting and his talent at playing many different roles, Antonio found it difficult to escape Hollywood's stereotyping of Hispanic actors as sex symbols.

to feeling "very Spanish. But at the same time I feel international, like I am from everywhere." That year, 1995, Antonio *was* seemingly everywhere, on movie marquees as well as in the tabloids.

5

GOING HOLLYWOOD

One day in 1995 while walking the streets of Los Angeles, Antonio spotted his name emblazoned on one movie marquee after another. He was stunned when he realized what was happening—he was being overexposed. Although excited to be offered roles, Antonio was doing exactly what he had been determined to avoid—to take his time and not constantly work.

Meanwhile, people at home in Spain were wondering if living in Hollywood had gone to Antonio's head. "I play games with that," Antonio confided to journalist Joe Rhodes. The actor told interviewers that when he's in Spain visiting, he jokes with friends who invite him to a party, asking if they are going to send a limo. When anyone back home starts treating him differently, he says, "*Stop* it, I am the guy who was playing soccer with you in the streets."

Seeing his friends and family in Spain always makes Antonio a little homesick for his native country. In Hollywood, business and money always seemed to be the

---

As Antonio's success exploded, he made several films that caused fans and friends to wonder if he was "going Hollywood" and doing films just to make money. Here, in his role as the gunman in Desperado, *he received acclaim for his acting and helped make up for the several box-office flops he made in the mid-1990s.*

main topics of conversation. In fact, money was at the forefront of a *People* magazine article about Antonio in 1996. They claimed the actor's box office receipts were a big disappointment. Antonio was now commanding $4 million per film, but for their money, studios were getting "a smoldering presence and a very un-Hollywood attitude about career management in return."

That attitude bucked the play-it-safe game plan followed by Hollywood. "I don't want to lose the capacity for failing or doing something bad," Antonio insisted to a journalist late in 1995. It looked as if failure was not haunting the actor, however. Earlier that year, Antonio had his first big hit.

Desperado was filmmaker Robert Rodriguez's studio-backed sequel to *El Mariachi*, a movie Rodriguez had made three years earlier for only $7,000. In both movies the main character is a musician on a mission of revenge after drug traffickers kill the woman he loves. A larger-than-life, cartoonish figure, he dresses all in black and carries around a guitar case full of guns.

Rodriguez wanted Antonio for his energy and his genuine quality. For his part, Antonio said, "I was interested because the part involved a lot of body work. I decided to think in terms of the choreography—to create the character from his body movement more than from the words he speaks." He added with a chuckle, "I probably borrowed more from flamenco dancers and bullfighters than from the Terminator."

Antonio's physical grace resulted in his doing most of his own stunts for *Desperado*, including inventing moves for one of the film's big shootout scenes. It was his idea to whip his arms around while gunning down a roomful of bad guys. He also came up with some lines of dialogue and even directed one sequence of the movie. In addition, Antonio played guitar himself and sang in the film. A video of one song featuring the actor appeared on the music television channel, MTV. The MTV audience was so impressed that they selected Antonio Most Desirable Male in 1996. (He shared the award in the Best Kiss category that year with *Desperado* costar Salma Hayek.)

Antonio's full-throttle performance in *Desperado* was a hit with critics as well as moviegoers. "The movie's a great showcase for Banderas's soulful, and soulfully funny, swashbuckling. He invests this action role with a flamenco dancer's grace and a brooding sensuality," declared *Newsweek* film critic David Ansen. *Harper's Bazaar* dubbed Antonio the "thinking woman's action hero."

Scoring a success with *Desperado* helped make up for the forgettable films Antonio appeared in that same year. In 1995 he could be seen as a hit man driven to replace the current top gun, played by Sylvester Stallone, in the big-budget release *Assassins*. He also costarred in the psychological thriller *Never Talk to Strangers* and the romantic comedy *Miami Rhapsody*. Plus, he had a part in the Robert Rodriguez–directed episode of the independent feature *Four Rooms*.

While his appearance in these box office duds did little to further his career, *Desperado* proved to Hollywood that Antonio was leading-man material. The film's profits showed that he could open a film—in other words, his name on the marquee could draw audiences. This quieted some fears in Hollywood that

American audiences would not accept a Spanish-born star.

Still, Hollywood worried over fan fallout from recent publicity regarding Antonio's private life. The media feeding frenzy was over the breakup of Antonio's marriage to Ana. In a situation straight out of the tabloids, the actor had fallen for a costar. In April 1995 he began filming the comedy *Two Much*, the story of a man pretending to be twins to pursue two different women. Antonio looked forward to the project for a couple of reasons. It was the first English-language feature directed by fellow countryman Fernando Trueba. Second, it was a chance to work with Melanie Griffith, an actress he admired. He still remembered what she was wearing— a white dress with pearls—when he met her for the first time at the Oscars in 1989.

Meeting Melanie again changed both their lives. Antonio admitted that he became infatuated by an image, as he explained:

> With Melanie, I liked her, and we were laughing together and spending some time and making jokes and talking about life between takes. And little by little, I was feeling more and more about this person. So we finish the movie, and we say, Well, bye! I was starting a new movie, and I thought this was probably an illusion that was going to go away. But it didn't. We started calling each other, then we saw each other, and I realized I was in love.

The tabloids gleefully reported the two celebrities were "an item." Melanie was already a recurring character in gossip columns. As the daughter of actress Tippi Hedren—star of the

Alfred Hitchcock chiller *The Birds*—Melanie had grown up in the glare of the media. Drugs, alcohol, and a roller-coaster relationship with actor Don Johnson all helped fuel gossip flames. She was still married to Johnson—for the second time—when she started her relationship with Antonio.

Antonio was still married too. He insists, though, that he and his wife were then living separate lives. He explained that he wanted to make American movies, and Ana did not. He claimed that his marriage was already broken when he fell in love with Melanie.

Despite Antonio's protests, the Spanish press portrayed his romance with a Hollywood celebrity as a betrayal of his Spanish roots as

In the film Two Much, *Antonio appeared with actress Melanie Griffith. When they met on the set and fell in love, their romance became an item for the gossip columns because both were married at the time. Despite the media frenzy, they refused to give each other up and married in 1996.*

well as his Spanish wife. At the same time, questions abounded concerning Antonio's reputation as a serious actor. Would the racy tabloid coverage damage the respect he had built up in the film industry?

For a time, it seemed as though the coverage would affect Antonio's life. United Nations International Children's Emergency Fund (UNICEF) turned down the actor's request to be sent to a current trouble spot, Sarajevo—even though he had represented the organization previously, in Somalia.

While expressing his understanding of UNICEF's position, Antonio still refused to give Melanie up. "I know there are people who would start thinking about me that I am being [too influenced] by Hollywood," he told *US* magazine. "But what would be really dirty is just to say, 'No, I am not gonna love this woman, because it would be bad for my career.' *That* is scary."

Antonio did, however, acknowledge the cost he was paying for the relationship. He admitted that others were implicated in the problem, including his family in Spain, his former wife, and Melanie's children. He did want to keep his personal story from becoming a media circus. While visiting in Spain, Antonio did his best to win over photographers by buying them cold drinks on a particularly hot day. He even managed to strike a deal with the paparazzi, the insistent photographers who followed the couple everywhere in Málaga. He asked that at least they give him and Melanie Tuesdays and Thursdays off.

Antonio may have arranged for some privacy when on vacation in Spain, but the media showed up in force when he and Melanie were

married on May 14, 1996. (Antonio's divorce had been finalized a month earlier while Melanie's had been granted in February.) To avoid the flash of camera lights and questions shouted by reporters, the couple's parents stayed away. The 15 wedding guests did, however, include Melanie's two children: Dakota, then 6, her daughter with Don Johnson; and Alexander, then 10, her son with actor Steven Bauer, her first husband. Before the ceremony ended, Alexander blurted out, "You may now kiss the bride!"

The half-hour ceremony took place in London, where Antonio was finishing filming *Evita*. The adaptation of the Andrew Lloyd

Visiting his home city of Málaga, Antonio saw friends and spent time at the beach. Accompanied by Melanie and her son, Alexander, the actor gives a cheerful thumbs up to the ever-present media.

With superstar Madonna in Evita, Antonio took on yet another role, that of a brooding revolutionary. In the film, Antonio proved that he could sing as well as act, further enhancing his reputation as a versatile performer.

Webber and Tim Rice musical starred Madonna in the title role. When shooting began in January of 1996, gossip columnists wondered whether Madonna would end up adding Antonio to her long list of romantic conquests. *Truth or Dare*, the 1991 "rockumentary" about the superstar, depicted the actress's frustration at finding Antonio arm-in-arm with his then wife, Ana, after anticipating meeting him at a party.

Antonio, however, has reportedly remained faithful to Melanie. His personal life was on an upswing, and the actor was also happy with his role in *Evita*. His character—modeled on the Latin American revolutionary hero Ché

Guevera—reminded Antonio of his own feelings while Spain was under the shadow of Francisco Franco. The mixed emotions Antonio had felt earlier at Franco's death helped him play his character's jumble of feelings toward the character of Evita, or Eva Perón, wife of Argentina's dictator Juan Perón in the 1940s and 1950s.

When Franco died in 1975, Antonio, then a teenager, almost cried when he heard the news. Later, in recalling his feelings, Antonio explained that while he hated the dictator, he was terribly saddened when he realized that not just a tyrant had passed on; an entire era in Spain had passed away with him.

Appearing in *Evita* brought back other memories for Antonio as well. When he was still dreaming of success, living in a boarding house in Madrid's theater district, a stage production of *Evita* played nightly nearby. "When I went to bed," Antonio says, "I could hear the music of *Evita*, the orchestra and everything."

With his next role, however, those memories of being a struggling actor were well behind Antonio. He was about to take the lead role in the smash summer hit *The Mask of Zorro*.

6

BEHIND THE CAMERA
AND BEYOND

Antonio's star performance in *The Mask of Zorro* sealed his position as one of Hollywood's sexiest leading men. At the same time, however, his ambitions were leading him away from acting in front of the camera to calling the shots behind it. With more than 15 years of acting experience, he was ready to try his hand at directing.

Critics questioned the Spanish actor's choice of projects for his debut as a director. He was taking on a movie based on Mark Childress's novel *Crazy in Alabama*. Told from the point of view of a 13-year-old boy named Peejoe, who is growing up in the American South, the story recounts how Peejoe's life is turned upside down when he witnesses injustices against African Americans in his small town in the mid-1960s.

In a commentary added to the DVD release of *Crazy in Alabama*, Antonio explained why he, as a foreigner, made a film about the 1960s civil rights movement in the United States. At the same time, he revealed his knowledge of Hollywood movie history. Antonio noted that ever since Hollywood's early years, foreign-born directors have told

---

In his new role as a director, Antonio peers into the camera to set up a scene. Although his first directorial debut, the film Crazy in Alabama, *was not a commercial success, he has not given up expanding his career into directing.*

American stories on film, mentioning that such famous filmmakers as Fritz Lang and Billy Wilder had been born in Europe.

Antonio also explained that his own experiences growing up under a dictatorship made him feel close to the characters in the story. They are all trying to achieve freedom in different ways, he said. Parallel to Peejoe's story, the film follows the adventures of the boy's aunt, Lucille, played by Melanie Griffith. Lucille has killed her physically abusive husband. She then leaves town to pursue her dream of stardom in Hollywood. As imagined by Peejoe, Aunt Lucille's trip west plays like a cartoon. Adding to the wackiness of her journey, she carries with her in a box the head of her dead husband.

A black comedy like *Crazy in Alabama* was a risky choice for his first project as a director, Antonio admitted to the *Los Angeles Times*. Critics generally felt he was unsuccessful in balancing the film's comic parts with the seriousness of the issues of civil rights and spousal abuse. Tom Gliatto's review for *People* read like many others. "The movie seesaws crazily: One second, Peejoe meets Martin Luther King Jr., the next, Aunt Lucille lands a guest spot on [the TV show] *Bewitched*," Gliatto wrote.

While movie reviewers shook their heads over *Crazy in Alabama*'s dizzying mood swings, the tabloids doubted that the couple's marriage would survive Antonio directing his new wife in the film. Antonio responded that working together only made their relationship closer. All he had to do was make eye contact with Melanie, and she would know immediately how Antonio wanted a scene played. Melanie explained, "Because Antonio is an actor, and a good one, he [knows] exactly how to

get something out of you in an easy way."
Costar Robert Wagner agrees: "He's an actor's
director—he reaches you."

For his part, Antonio commented how his
experience as an actor helped him as a director:
"There were times as an actor when I could not
bring out certain emotions, and I recognized
that was happening with some of the actors.
So, directing gave me a chance to play with
feelings and push some buttons that helped
the actors perform."

Besides coaxing to get the performances he
wanted from his actors, Antonio admitted that
directing involves behaving like an answering
machine—that is, fielding questions all day
long from the cast and crew. To make it easier
for him to answer questions about technical
matters, Antonio hired a Spanish-speaking
production team. Although all lived in the United
States at the time, the film's cinematographer,
Julio Macat, was originally from Argentina; the
costume designer, Graciela Mazon, was from
Mexico; and the set designer, Cecile Monticl,
came from Peru. Another reason Antonio hired
them was because their experience on foreign
films (which are often made inexpensively)
taught them to work creatively within a tight
budget.

Crazy in Alabama's budget—under $20 million
—was relatively small for a Hollywood film in
1999. Still, it lost money. On its opening week-
end, the film barely brought in $1 million. The
film's bomb at the box office ended up burning
Antonio financially as well. It was, after all, the
first feature produced by Green Moon, a production company he had started with Melanie.
Crazy in Alabama's disappointing reviews and
poor box office showing failed, however, to

dampen Antonio's enthusiasm for directing. "I discovered that I have a real knack for the visual—something I never knew before," he told the *Los Angeles Times*. "I think I am going to keep developing this, if possible."

In fact, hours before *Crazy in Alabama*'s world premiere at the Venice Film Festival in September 1999, Antonio announced his next project behind the camera for Green Moon. The film, an adaptation of the book *Málaga Burning: An American Woman's Eyewitness Account of the Spanish Civil War*, would be a very personal one. First of all, the events take place in Antonio's hometown of Málaga. Also, Antonio's mother had told him about Spain's civil war as the background to her girlhood in the 1930s. Stories she told him about people being killed and tortured were burned into his memory. Again, Antonio was involving himself in a film about the struggle for freedom.

For Antonio, directing *Málaga Burning* would also be a way of returning to his roots. The project therefore fulfills a promise he made when receiving the Imagen Foundation's Lasting Image Award in April 1999. Antonio quoted a line from *The Mambo Kings* to the packed house at the awards ceremony honoring positive images of Latinos and Latino culture— "A man without roots is nobody"—and he added, "I will never lose mine."

But before returning to his Spanish roots in directing *Málaga Burning*, Antonio had acting commitments to fulfill. In the 1999 release *The 13th Warrior*, he played a 10th-century Arab poet recruited to help fight a fearsome tribe that eats its enemies. The role won Antonio the outstanding actor honor the following spring at the American Latino Media

Arts Awards. It was his second straight ALMA win. In 1999, he had picked up an acting award for his performance in *The Mask of Zorro*. And, at the awards ceremony in April 2000, a genuinely surprised Antonio was honored as a director—for *Crazy in Alabama*—as well as an actor. Sweeping both the acting and directing categories, Antonio set an ALMA award record that night.

Antonio's second movie of 1999, *Play It to the Bone*, cast him as a Madrid-born boxer. In the movie's big fight scene, costar Woody Harrelson accidentally broke Antonio's nose. The actor proudly showed off the injury to journalist Louise Farr, saying, "You carry whatever happens to you in life. I don't want to fix anything." Farr sensed that leaving his nose broken was Antonio's way of defying Hollywood's packaging of him as a Latin heartthrob.

Indeed, Antonio's choice of roles continues to make it harder to typecast him. In December 1999 he finished shooting *The Body* in Jerusalem and other locations in Israel. In the film he plays a Roman Catholic priest investigating an archaeologist's discovery of bones that may be those of Jesus. What attracted him to the part was not only an opportunity to distance himself from his sex-symbol image. The role also challenged him to downplay his physical grace and expressiveness as an actor. Portraying a character whose life is intensely inward would give him a chance to try out internal acting techniques he learned from Oscar-winner Anthony Hopkins, his costar in *The Mask of Zorro*.

Making *The Body* also risked Antonio's physical safety. The Israeli government, as well as the film's production company, supplied bodyguards for his protection. The tensions simmering among Jerusalem's religious communities were always threatening to break out into violence. Adding to the unease as the year 2000 neared was the end-of-the-world hysteria centering on the city, holy to three of the world's major faiths.

The first week of December 1999, Antonio took a brief break from the pressures of shooting *The Body* to fly to Berlin and attend the European Film Awards. At the ceremony, he and director Roman Polanski were honored with an award for Achievement in World Cinema. In addition, Antonio presented Pedro Almodóvar with the European Film of the Year Award for Almodóvar's hugely popular *All About My Mother*. Caught up in the emotion of the moment, Antonio dropped to his knees to hold the award up to his friend and mentor.

At home now in both European and American productions, the globe-trotting actor was set to appear again in the film version of another British stage musical. The first time he sang and acted the part of Ché in Andrew Lloyd Webber's *Evita*. This time he would be playing the title role in Andrew Lloyd Webber's *Phantom of the Opera.*

Antonio was taking a big chance starring in a role closely identified with another actor. As the original theatrical Phantom, Michael Crawford had created a buzz playing to audiences all over the world. To audition for the part, Antonio traveled to London for Lloyd Webber's 50th birthday celebration in April 1998. Before an audience of 4,000 at the Royal Albert Hall, the actor performed tunes from *Phantom* as well as *Evita*. Lloyd Webber was so impressed by Antonio's performance that he called Warner Brothers, the studio making the *Phantom of*

the Opera, and convinced them to sign Antonio right away. The actor promises he will put his soul into the project, and he even vowed to quit smoking to better perform all the singing the role of the Phantom demands.

Referring to the white mask the Phantom wears and the black one worn by Zorro, Antonio joked, "I'll be the only actor in Hollywood who went from wearing a black mask to wearing a white mask." In fact, Antonio will be putting the black mask on again soon. He has agreed to star in a sequel to *The Mask of Zorro*, which also will be produced by Steven Spielberg.

First, however, he will be seen in the steamy thriller *Original Sin*, with Oscar-winning actress Angelina Jolie. For a change of pace, Antonio will also appear in the children's adventure *Spy*

For his international work, in 1999 Antonio was awarded the European Contribution to World Cinema by the European Film Academy. He shared the stage and the honors with Spanish actress Cecilia Roth and Pedro Almodóvar (center), with whom Antonio has remained friends and colleagues since their first film together.

Kids. A film by *Desperado* writer-director Robert Rodriguez, *Spy Kids* follows a pair of kids on a mission to rescue their secret-agent parents. In the movie, described by Rodriguez as a cross between James Bond and Willie Wonka, Antonio plays the kids' father. Antonio said he is pleased to be in a film he can take his young daughter, Stella, to see.

Stella del Carmen Banderas-Griffith was born September 24, 1996, in Marbella, Spain, less than 20 miles from Antonio's birthplace of Málaga. The name Stella means "star" in Latin, and Carmen, Antonio explained, signifies the patron saint of sailors in the south of Spain— a nod to Antonio's love of sailing.

Dad and mom both recall the day Stella was born. "I had to climb over the wall," Melanie says, laughing about sneaking past a crowd of photographers to the local hospital, "because we couldn't go out the front gate." Also laughing, Antonio adds, "We had a rental car waiting, and we covered ourselves with a blanket in the back seat." Growing serious, he says, "That night was the happiest night of my life."

The proud papa says Stella speaks both English and Spanish. She and her parents holiday as much as possible in Marbella to be near Antonio's family. When visiting Spain, they stay in a home near the Mediterranean Sea. Antonio and Melanie also own a home in Los Angeles. The house is built in the Mediterranean style—tile roofs and floors and stucco walls. Before moving in, the couple remodeled the house to include a sauna, gym, and music studio. Living with them and Stella in Los Angeles are Melanie's two kids, Alexander and Dakota.

Antonio admitted that at first it was hard

His daughter, Stella, in his arms, Antonio shares the spotlight with Melanie and her son, Alexander. A devoted husband and father to his family, Antonio cherishes his happy personal life. Even with his huge success and celebrity status, he is determined to keep it that way.

having a mixed family. "We had to talk—mostly with Alexander." He said to the boy, who was 10 at the time, "Tell me exactly what you think, and don't think I'm gonna get mad at you. I want to try to understand everything that's happening in your mind. Because I've been a kid, too, and I know how painful it is sometimes." Antonio considers himself a parent to Dakota and Alexander as well as to Stella. He says he and Melanie "both feel that our family is our center and that our love for each other and our children will keep us happy and strong."

The couple's fourth wedding anniversary, May 14, 2000, ended up being a double celebration for the family. That day, Antonio received an honorary doctor of arts degree from Dickinson College in Pennsylvania, which recognized Antonio for his theater and film work in Spain, as well as his crossing cultural and language borders to build a career in the United States. The actor was chosen as a model for students on risk-taking in the world of the arts and also as an example of being able to triumph in a global environment.

In his acceptance speech, Antonio stated he was especially honored as the first Spanish actor to be awarded this special degree. He also said he planned to work again soon in his native country. He confirmed that he would be appearing in an upcoming film by director Pedro Almodóvar.

Whether pursuing his ambition to make movies or making decisions concerning his personal life, Antonio says he does not set fixed goals for himself. "Instead I like to remind myself of a poem by the Spanish poet Antonio Machado. Loosely translated, he wrote: 'There is no path. You make the path when you walk.' And that is how I live my life—never accepting the easy route but always forging my own way."

CHRONOLOGY

1960	Born José Antonio Dominguez on August 10 in Málaga, Spain.
1976	Enrolls at the School of Dramatic Art in Málaga.
1980	Graduates from drama school and moves to Spain's capital, Madrid, to pursue an acting career.
1981	Accepts membership in the acting company of Spain's National Theater.
1982	Makes his screen debut in *Labyrinth of Passion*, a film by Pedro Almodóvar; changes name to Antonio Banderas.
1988	Marries fellow Spanish actor Ana Leza; attracts the attention of Hollywood in Almodóvar's *Women on the Verge of a Nervous Breakdown*.
1992	Makes his American film debut in *The Mambo Kings*.
1995	Appears in five U.S. films, including his first starring role for American audiences in *Desperado*.
1996	Wins MTV Award for Most Desirable Male and shares an award for Best Kiss with *Desperado* costar Selma Hayak; marries American actress Melanie Griffith on May 14; daughter Stella del Carmen Banderas-Griffith born on September 24; nominated for a Golden Globe for Best Actor in a Comedy or Musical for *Evita*.
1998	Proves a box office attraction in the summer blockbuster *The Mask of Zorro*; nominated for a Golden Globe Best Actor in a Comedy or Musical for the film.
1999	Wins ALMA Award as outstanding actor for *The Mask of Zorro*; premieres *Crazy in Alabama*, his directorial debut and the first feature film released by Green Moon, his production company with wife Melanie; accepts European Achievement in World Cinema Award at Venice Film Festival on December 4.
2000	Named both outstanding actor and outstanding director at the fifth annual ALMA Awards on April 16; receives an honorary doctorate from Pennsylvania's Dickinson College on May 14.

FILMOGRAPHY

1982   *Laberinto de pasiones/Labyrinth of Passion*
           Pestañas postizas

1983   *El Caso Almería*
           El Señor Galindez
           Y del seguro . . . libranos señor!

1984   *Los zancos*

1985   *La corte del faraón*
           Réquiem por un campesino español

1986   *Así como habian sido*
           Delirios de amor
           Matador
           The Puzzle
           27 horas

1987   *La ley del deseo/Law of Desire*
           El placer de matar

1988   *Bajarse al moro*
           Bâton rouge
           Mujeres al borde de un ataque de nervios/
               Women on the Verge of a Nervous Breakdown

1989   *La paloma blanca*
           La mujer de tu vida: La mujer feliz
           Si te dicen que caí

1990   *Átame!/Tie Me Up! Tie Me Down!*
           Contra el viento

1991   *Cuentos de Borges I*
           Terra Nova
           Una mujer bajo la lluvia

1992   *The Mambo Kings*

1993   *Dispara!*
           Giovane Mussolini, II
           The House of the Spirits
           Philadelphia

1994	*Interview with the Vampire*
	Of Love and Shadows

1995	*Assassins*
	Desperado
	Four Rooms
	Miami Rhapsody
	Never Talk to Strangers

1996	*Evita*
	Two Much

| 1998 | *The Mask of Zorro* |

1999	*Crazy in Alabama* (director)
	Play It to the Bone
	The 13th Warrior

2000	*The Body*
	Original Sin

| 2001 | *Spy Kids* |

AWARDS

| 1996 | MTV Award for Most Desirable Male |

1999	European Achievement in World Cinema Award
	ALMA Award for Outstanding Actor in a Feature Film, *The Mask of Zorro*
	Imagen Foundation's Lasting Image Award

2000	ALMA Award for Outstanding Actor in a Feature Film, *The 13th Warrior*
	ALMA Outstanding Director of a Feature Film, *Crazy in Alabama*

FURTHER READING

Ansen, David. "A Neo-Latin Lover." *Newsweek*, September 4, 1995.

Bart, Peter. *The Gross: The Hits, The Flops—The Summer That Ate Hollywood*. New York: St. Martin's Press, 1999.

Grabowski, John F. *Spain*. San Diego: Lucent Books, 2000.

Hawkes, Ellen. "The Day Antonio Found His Passion." *Parade* magazine, October 10, 1999.

Johnson, Hillary. "My Antonio." *Harper's Bazaar*, August 1995.

Keller, Gary D. *Hispanics and United States Film: An Overview and Handbook*. Tempe, Ariz.: Bilingual Press, 1994.

Reyes, Luis, and Peter Rubie. *Hispanics in Hollywood: An Encyclopedia of Film and Television*. New York: Garland, 1994.

Tracy, Kathleen. *Antonio Banderas*. New York: St. Martin's Press Paperbacks, 1996.

INDEX

Almodóvar, Pedro, 24-26, 28, 54, 58

Assassins, 41

Bandera, Ana (mother), 15, 18, 19, 21

Banderas, Antonio
   and American film debut, 31
   awards received by, 26, 41, 52-53, 54, 58
   birth of, 16
   childhood of, 15-19
   children of, 45, 56-58
   and decision to become actor, 17-19
   as director, 49-52, 53
   education of, 16, 19
   family of, 15
   and honorary doctorate, 58
   in Madrid, 21, 23-24
   marriages of. *See* Griffith, Melanie; Leza, Ana
   and name change, 25
   and theater, 19-21, 25, 26

Banderas-Griffith, Stella del Carmen (daughter), 56

Belaguer, Luis, 21

Body, The, 53-54

Crazy in Alabama (director), 49-52, 53

Demme, Jonathan, 33-34

Desperado, 40-41

Dickinson College, 58

Dintel, 19-21

Dominguez, José (father), 15, 19

Evita, 45-47, 54

Feuer, Howard, 34

Franco, Francisco, 16, 19-20, 23, 35, 47, 50

Glimcher, Arne, 31-32, 33, 34

Green Moon (production company), 51, 52

Griffith, Melanie (second wife), 42-46, 50-51, 56-58

House of the Spirits, The, 35

Interview with the Vampire, 36

Labyrinth of Passion, 25

Leza, Ana (first wife), 27-28, 42, 43, 45, 46

Machado, Antonio, 58

Málaga Burning (director), 52

Mambo Kings Play Songs of Love, The, 31-33, 35, 52

Mask of Zorro, The, 7-12, 49, 53, 57

Mask of Zorro, The (sequel), 55

Matador, 25

Miami Rhapsody, 41

Movida, La ("The Movement"), 23, 24

MTV, 41

National Theater, 24, 26

Never Talk to Strangers, 41

Original Sin, 55

Pasqual, Luis, 24

Phantom of the Opera, 54-55

Philadelphia, 33-34

Play It to the Bone, 53

Rice, Tim, 46

Rodriguez, Robert, 40, 41, 56

School of Dramatic Art, 19

Solo, Guillermina, 19

Spielberg, Steven, 7, 55

Spy Kids, 55-56

13th Warrior, The, 52-53

Tie Me Up! Tie Me Down!, 26

Two Much, 42

Webber, Andrew Lloyd, 45-46, 54-55

Women on the Verge of a Nervous Breakdown, 28

ABOUT THE AUTHOR

AMY ALLISON attended junior high school in the same Los Angeles neighborhood where Antonio Banderas and his family now have a home. She currently lives in another part of the city with her husband, Dave. Allison's other biography for Chelsea House, *Roger Williams*, tells the story of the founder of Rhode Island—a risk-taker like Antonio. Allison has also written *Shakespeare's Globe*, a recounting of one of the world's most famous theaters. Her poems have appeared in *Cricket* magazine.